YOU HAVE A PET WHAT?!

FERRET

Cristie Reed

Rourke
Educational Media

rourkeeducationalmedia.com

Scan for Related Titles
and Teacher Resources

Before Reading:

Building Academic Vocabulary and Background Knowledge

Before reading a book, it is important to tap into what your child or students already know about the topic. This will help them develop their vocabulary, increase their reading comprehension, and make connections across the curriculum.

1. *Look at the cover of the book. What will this book be about?*
2. *What do you already know about the topic?*
3. *Let's study the Table of Contents. What will you learn about in the book's chapters?*
4. *What would you like to learn about this topic? Do you think you might learn about it from this book? Why or why not?*
5. *Use a reading journal to write about your knowledge of this topic. Record what you already know about the topic and what you hope to learn about the topic.*
6. *Read the book.*
7. *In your reading journal, record what you learned about the topic and your response to the book.*
8. *After reading the book complete the activities below.*

Content Area Vocabulary
Read the list. What do these words mean?

bedding

canine

carnivores

descendants

disinfected

domesticated

inquisitive

kibble

musky

neutering

After Reading:

Comprehension and Extension Activity

After reading the book, work on the following questions with your child or students in order to check their level of reading comprehension and content mastery.

1. *The word ferret comes from a Latin word meaning little thief. How does the ferret live up to its name? (Infer)*
2. *Why is it important to research possible pets prior to adopting them into your family? (Asking questions)*
3. *Do you think a ferret is a good pet for you? Explain. (Text to self connection)*
4. *What are some ways ferrets have helped people? (Asking questions)*
5. *In what ways are ferrets similar to cats and dogs? (Summarize)*

Extension Activity
The black-footed ferret is an endangered relative of the domestic ferret. Research the black-footed ferret and create a plan of action to bring awareness to this endangered species. Share your plan with your class or family.

Table of Contents

Weaseling Its Way into Your Heart

Have you ever heard of the weasel war dance? Have you ever been scared by a sofa monster? Have you ever encountered a carpet shark? Does the crocodile roll sound like fun? Meet the funny, furry little critter that can show you all of these tricks: the ferret.

FUN FACT

When ferrets get excited and want to play, they hop sideways, leap, and bounce. Ferret owners call this the weasel war dance.

Ferrets are mammals and part of the weasel family. This family includes minks, otters, badgers, wolverines, and polecats. Only ferrets are kept as pets. Ferrets are **carnivores** and closely related to skunks. Like their stinky relatives, ferrets have scent glands under their tail. They give off a bad smell to scare away enemies.

Mink

Otter

Wolverine

Badger

Black-footed ferret

FUN FACT

The black-footed ferret is a wild relative of the domesticated ferret. It is an endangered species that lives in the western United States.

Ferrets' bodies are long, strong, and flexible. Their strength and flexibility comes from having unusually long vertebrae in their spines. Their bodies are supported by short legs that allow them to crawl through small spaces. They have straight tails and each foot has five toes with claws.

round eyes

pointy nose

triangular head

34 sharp teeth

small rounded ears

long whiskers

Ferrets have triangular shaped heads. They have small, rounded ears, round eyes, a pointy nose, and long whiskers. Ferrets have 34 sharp teeth, including four **canine** teeth like dogs and cats. Their eyesight is somewhat poor, but they are equipped with an excellent sense of smell and keen hearing.

FUN FACT

kits: baby ferrets
hobs: adult males
jills: adult females
business: group of ferrets
hoblet: neutered male
sprite: spayed female

long vertebrae in spine

straight tail

five toes
with claws

short legs

Unlike cats and dogs, there is only one breed of domestic ferret. But within that breed, ferrets vary in coat color and markings. A ferret may have a mask across its face, a bib of color on its chest, or a blaze of color down its back. Some ferrets have a color pattern similar to a panda. Their fluffy coats have two layers: outer protective hairs and an undercoat.

FUN FACT

The word ferret comes from a Latin word, furittus, which means little thief.

Ferret Colors

Ferret Colors	Guard Colors	Undercoat	Eyes	Nose	Photo
albino	white to cream	white to cream	ruby red	pink	
black	true black	white or slight golden	black	solid or speckled black	
black sable	dark blackish brown	white to cream	dark brown or black	solid or speckled blackish brown	
champagne	tan or light chocolate	white to cream	dark brown or black	beige, pink, or pink with a beige or light brown t-outline	
chocolate	milk chocolate brown	white or slight golden	brown or burgundy	pink, beige, brick, or with a light brown t-outline	
dark-eyed white	white to cream	white to cream	burgundy	pink	
sable	warm, deep brown	white, cream, or light golden	brown or black	light brown, speckled brown, or with a brown t-outline	

The Ferret's Place in History

Ferrets are not wild animals. They were **domesticated** about 2,500 years ago. Scientists believe they are **descendants** of the European polecat. People started keeping ferrets thousands of years ago in ancient Greece. They used them for ferreting other small animals out of their holes. Ferrets could catch small game or chase it into the hands of a waiting hunter.

◀◀ *Ferreting with muzzled ferrets is described in* Livre de Chasse, *or* Book of the Hunt, *written by Count Gaston Phoebus of France in 1387.*

When people traveled from Europe to the New World, ferrets came along on ships to kill mice. In North America, people started keeping ferrets in the 17th century. Wherever grain was stored, rodents came to feast. Ferrets helped eliminate pesky rats and mice.

The pet ferret fad started in the United States in the 1980s. People liked their small size and playful personalities. They could be kept in small spaces and trained to use litter boxes.

Genghis Khan circa 1227

Frederick II 1194-1250

FUN FACT

Ferrets have a royal connection. German Emperor Frederick II and Mongolian leader Ghengis Khan kept ferrets for hunting.

A Ferret Life for Me

Ferrets are small and quiet like cats. They are playful and affectionate like dogs. They have funny, lovable personalities. They dance around, pounce on shoes, play hide-and-seek, and chase anything that rolls. Their energy can seem limitless.

Ferrets play hard and sleep hard. They need between 15 and 20 hours of sleep each day. They sleep so deeply you might wonder if they are still alive! They typically sleep for a few hours, wake up, eat, go to the bathroom, play, then sleep some more.

FUN FACT

More about Hobs and Jills
Male ferrets are always bigger than female ferrets.
- **weight**: females 1-3 pounds (0.5-1.4 kilograms); males 3-5 pounds (1.4-2.3 kilograms)
- **length**: females 12-16 inches (30-41 centimeters); males 16-24 inches (41-61 centimeters)
- **lifespan:** females 6-10 years; males 7-10 years

The **inquisitive** ferret likes to crawl into small spaces. Drawers, shopping bags, and boxes are favorite hiding places. Ferrets have some mischievous ways. They like to take small objects or toys and hide them. Owners fondly call them sofa monsters and carpet sharks because they like to hide in sofa cushions and crawl under rugs.

Ferrets speak a unique language. A soft barking noise referred to as dooking is its happy sound. A scared ferret will hiss. An upset ferret will squeak or scream.

Ferrets love and need attention from their owners. They become very attached to their humans. They also enjoy playing games and sleeping with other ferrets.

Ferrets can become friends with cats and dogs. They are natural hunters, so small pets such as hamsters, gerbils, and reptiles should not be kept around ferrets.

The Right Pet?

Kits start their lives as part of a litter of six to ten baby ferrets. They are blind, deaf, and have no teeth. Like other mammals, they drink milk from their mother. Kits can leave their mother when they are between eight and 12 weeks old.

As new pets, kits need lots of time and attention. They begin to bond with their humans and learn their role in the family. Kits sleep a lot! When not sleeping, they will play and play.

A newborn ferret is so small it can fit into a tablespoon. All kits have white fur when they are born. ▶▶

Ferrets in the Family

Ferrets need to live indoors. They prefer a cool area and a comfy cage. Cages should be large enough to provide a sleeping area and eating area. They also need a bathroom area. Ferrets can live by themselves, in pairs, or with a group.

Their sleeping area should have soft **bedding**. They like a place to hang out, such as a hammock.

Their eating area needs a sturdy food dish and a water bottle. Ferrets are meat eaters like cats and dogs. They eat a dry **kibble** that provides lots of protein. For treats, ferrets can eat cooked turkey or chicken. Ferrets need to eat frequently and they need lots of fresh water.

Train your ferret to use a water bottle. They like to play in water, so having a bowl could get messy!

Pet Pointers

Fruits and vegetables should not be fed to a ferret. They are unable to digest any food that comes from plants.

Ferrets can be trained to use a litter box. The bathroom area should be away from the eating and sleeping areas. They eat a lot and go a lot! Their litter must be cleaned often.

The ferret's cage should be cleaned and **disinfected** weekly. Bedding and bowls need to be washed. This prevents sickness and helps control odors.

Pet Pointers

A healthy ferret has a thick, glossy coat. It has long whiskers and white teeth. Its eyes are bright and alert. Its nose is moist. It has a good disposition. It is alert, curious, and playful.

Important responsibilities go along with owning any pet. Just like dogs and cats, ferrets need care that is suited to their needs.

A happy, healthy ferret needs plenty of exercise and attention from its owner. Ferrets need to be out of their cages every day for four to six hours of exercise. They need playtime with their humans to go for walks and learn new tricks.

▶▶ *Ferrets like to hide in small places, like a pocket, and crawl through tubes and tunnels.*

Ferrets naturally have a light **musky** smell. This comes from glands in their skin. Clean bedding and a healthy diet help eliminate odor. Spaying or **neutering** also makes them less smelly. A bath every couple of months helps, too.

Pet Pointers
A veterinarian may need to perform an operation to remove a ferret's scent glands.

Veterinarians help keep ferrets healthy throughout their lives. Ferrets need to visit the veterinarian twice a year. The doctor will check their teeth to see if they need cleaning and check their ears for mites. Ferrets need yearly vaccinations against rabies and distemper. A veterinarian helps keep ferrets free of fleas and ticks.

Pet Pointers

Ferret Care
- Clean ears every two to three weeks
- Trim nails every two to three weeks
- Check teeth twice a year
- Get a bath every one to two months

Ferret Feats

The friendly ferret can learn to do fun tricks. They love to hear their names and will come when called. They can be taught to sit up on their hind legs, play dead, and roll over — much like a dog. Ferrets can learn to walk on a leash attached to a special harness.

walking on a leash

tuck and scoot

sitting up

crocodile roll

Many owners train their ferret to come when it hears a squeaky sound. They squeak a toy and reward the ferret for coming. It is important to teach them to come because they like to hide and it can be hard to find them.

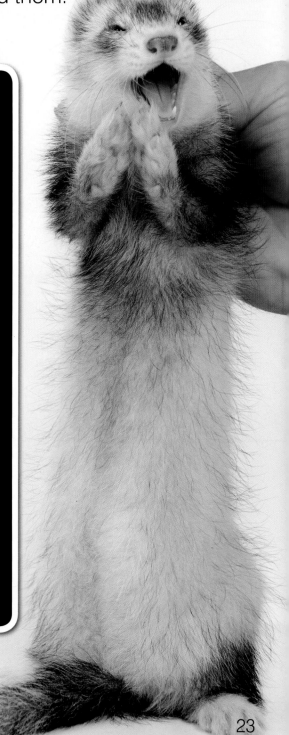

Do You Speak Ferret?

Ferret owners speak a special language. How many ferret expressions do you know?

Blow a bomb: a startled ferret sprays with its scent glands

Couch sharking: a ferret hides in sofa cushions and jumps out to scare someone

Dance of joy: what a ferret does when it is happy to see someone

Doughnut: sleeping in a circle

Ferret juggling: trying to hold an active ferret

Hidey-hole: a place where ferrets hide

S.N.D.: stands for "sleeping not dead" — the deep sleep of a ferret

Training a ferret requires kindness and a gentle manner. Positive reinforcement works best. When they do something you want them to do, let them know it with a pat or a kiss.

Ferrets like to be rewarded with special treats such as a bit of egg. They also like to be rewarded with a favorite toy. Use praise and a positive tone of voice.

When your ferret misbehaves, let it know. Use a firm voice and say, "No!" Give it a timeout in a pet carrier. You can also correct misbehavior by picking it up by the loose skin on the back of its neck. This is called scruffing.

Use your thumb and first few fingers to hold your ferret firmly enough to immobilize it but not enough to hurt your pet.

Ferret Power

Ferrets can perform an unusual function. Some have been trained to lead wires and cables through confined spaces to help with aircraft manufacturing and building construction. Lines are attached to their harnesses. They run along through narrow spaces or tunnels pulling lines along with them.

No Ferrets Allowed?!

Cities and states have different laws about ferret ownership. At one time, ferrets were classified as wild animals that could not be legally kept as pets. Some of those laws still exist, but many restrictions have changed and ferret ownership is more widely accepted. Most places still require permits to breed ferrets.

Ferret ownership is illegal in California and Hawaii. California's Fish and Game Commission places them on a restrictive wildlife list. In Hawaii they are considered possible carriers of the rabies virus. Some cities such as Washington, D.C. and New York City restrict ferret ownership.

Does your city or state have laws about ferret ownership?

Pet Pointers

If you decide to add a ferret to your family, consider adopting one from an animal rescue organization.

Things to Think About
If You Want a Pet Ferret

- A ferret owner must be willing to devote a lot of time to their pet.
- Ferrets can be smelly. They naturally give off a musky odor.
- Ferrets may nip their owners to get their attention or when they are startled.
- A ferret's home needs to be ferret-proofed to eliminate the places it could hide and get lost.
- Ferrets like to steal things and hide them. Small objects should be kept out of their reach.
- Ferrets like to chew. They can cause damage with their sharp teeth.
- Ferrets have difficulty living in temperatures above 85 degrees Fahrenheit (29 degrees Celsius).
- Ferrets need close supervision when they are out of their cages.
- Because of their body type and high activity level, a ferret may be difficult for a young child to handle.
- Ferrets can't be around smaller animals such as rabbits, hamsters, gerbils, and small reptiles.
- Ferrets have some unusual health problems. They are prone to some kinds of cancer. They can catch and transmit the flu.

Glossary

bedding (BED-ing): material used for animals to cushion their bodies and absorb smells and wetness

canine (KAY-nine): pointed teeth on each side of the upper and lower jaw

carnivores (KAR-nuh-vorz): animals that eat meat

descendants (di-SEND-uhntz): those who can be traced to a particular individual or group

disinfected (diss-in-FEKT-id): cleaned for the purpose of killing germs

domesticated (duh-MESS-tuh-kate-id): tamed to live with or used by humans

inquisitive (in-KWIZ-i-tiv): extremely curious

kibble (KIB-uhl): coarsely ground dry food for animals

musky (MUHS-kee): an unpleasant animal odor

neutering (NOO-tur-een): a medical procedure that prevents male animals from reproducing

Index

Show What You Know

1. What makes a ferret unique?

2. What responsibilities are required in the day-to-day care of a pet ferret?

3. How can you keep a ferret healthy throughout its lifetime?

4. Ferrets have been kept by humans for different reasons over the course of history. Identify the reasons and explain how ferret ownership has changed over time.

5. What are the benefits and challenges of having a ferret for a pet?

Websites to Visit

www.humanesociety.org/animals/ferrets

www.a-z-animals.com/animals/ferret

www.ferret.org/read/faq.html

About the Author

Cristie Reed is a literacy teacher and lifelong animal lover. She enjoys caring for pets. In her lifetime she has owned and cared for three pet goats, a few chickens, a few ducks, a green snake, two anole lizards, a guinea pig, a pony, a caiman, a squirrel, three cats, eight dogs, and one very special peacock. She lives in Florida with her husband and miniature schnauzer, Rocky.

Meet The Author!
www.meetREMauthors.com

PHOTO CREDITS: Cover: ©Porbeagle; page 1: ©Dauma; page 3, page 30: Denis Kukareko; page 4, page 9(a): ©Fotojagodka; page 5 (top left): ©Frank Leung; page 5 (top right): ©dstong; page 5 (middle left): ©Anna Yu; page 5 (middle right): ©John Pitcher; page 5 (right bottom), page 10, page 11: Wikipedia; page 6-7, page 9 (a): ©Astakova; page 8, page 9 (d,f,g), page 22 (right): ©Eric Isselee; page 9 (c): ©dien; page 9 (e), page 18 (top): ©Couperfield; page 11 (bottom): ©mimic51; page 11(bottom): ©Pakhnyushchyy; page 12, page 17 (bottom), page 25: ©Cycnoclub; page 13: ©Deborah Aronds; page 14: ©Juergen Bosse; page 15: ©Radkate; page 16: ©Adya; page 17: ©marilyna; page 18: ©Jagodka; page 18 (bottom), page 26 (left): ©IrinaK; page 18(bottom): ©JoSchwlo; page 19: ©Pecak; page 20: ©Andrey Snegirev; page 21: ©Antov Gvozdikov; page 22 (top): ©Tom Lester; page 22 (middle left): ©Ermolaev Alexander; page 22 (bottom): ©StudioDMM; page 23: ©Inna Astakhova; page 24: ©nanka; page 25: ©Meisone; page 26: ©CS333; page 27: ©Eurobanks; page 28: ©Profesor25

Edited by: Keli Sipperley

Cover design and Interior design by: Rhea Magaro

Library of Congress PCN Data

Ferret / Cristie Reed
(You Have a Pet What?!)
ISBN 978-1-63430-432-0 (hard cover)
ISBN 978-1-63430-532-7 (soft cover)
ISBN 978-1-63430-621-8 (e-Book)
Library of Congress Control Number: 2015931855

Printed in the United States of America, North Mankato, Minnesota

Also Available as:

ROURKE'S e-Books